NATIONAL
GEOGRAPHIC

T0045270

I Work at Night

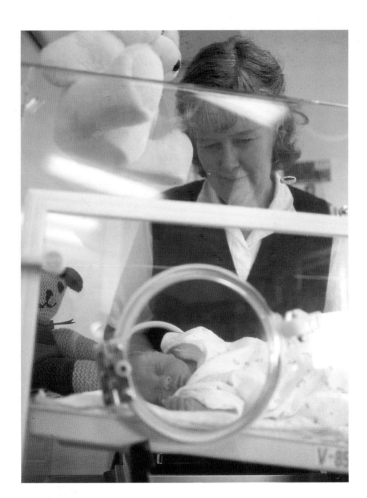

Leroy Taylor

I work at night.
I bake bread.

baker

2

I work at night.
I clean offices.

cleaning woman

3

driver

I work at night.
I drive a truck.

I work at night.
I serve food.

server

street cleaner

I work at night.
I clean streets.

6

I work at night.
I help people.

nurse

7

Picture Index